~A BINGO BOOK~

Pennsylvania Bingo Book

COMPLETE BINGO GAME IN A BOOK

Written By Rebecca Stark

ISBN 978-0-87386-531-9

Educational Books 'n' Bingo

Printed in the U.S.A.

DIRECTIONS

INCLUDED:

List of Terms

Templates for Additional Terms and Clues

2 Clues per Term

30 Unique Bingo Cards

Markers

1. **Either cut apart the book or make copies of ALL the sheets. You might want to make an extra copy of the clue sheets to use for introduction and review. Keep the sheets in an envelope for easy reuse.**

2. Cut apart the call cards with terms and clues.

3. Pass out one bingo card per student. There are enough for a class of 30.

4. Pass out markers. You may cut apart the markers included in this book or use any other small items of your choice.

5. Decide whether or not you will require the entire card to be filled. Requiring the entire card to be filled provides a better review. However, if you have a short time to fill, you may prefer to have them do the just the border or some other format. Tell the class before you begin what is required.

6. There are 50 terms. Read the list before you begin. If there are any terms that have not been covered in class, you may want to read to the students the term and clues before you begin.

7. There is a blank space in the middle of each card. You can instruct the students to use it as a free space or you can write in answers to cover terms not included. Of course, in this case you would create your own clues. (Templates provided.)

8. Shuffle the cards and place them in a pile. Two or three clues are provided for each term. If you plan to play the game with the same group more than once, you might want to choose a different clue for each game. If not, you may choose to use more than one clue.

9. Be sure to keep the cards you have used for the present game in a separate pile. When a student calls, "Bingo," he or she will have to verify that the correct answers are on his or her card AND that the markers were placed in response to the proper questions. Pull out the cards that are on the student's card keeping them in the order they were used in the game. Read each clue as it was given and ask the student to identify the correct answer from his or her card.

10. If the student has the correct answers on the card AND has shown that they were marked in response to the *correct questions,* then that student is the winner and the game is over. If the student does not have the correct answers on the card OR he or she marked the answers in response to *the wrong questions,* then the game continues until there is a proper winner.

11. If you want to play again, reshuffle the cards and begin again.

Have fun!

TERMS INCLUDED

Allegheny Plateau

Allentown

Atlantic Coastal Plain

Battle of Gettysburg

Border(s)

James Buchanan

Commonwealth

County (-ies)

Crop(s)

Declaration of Independence

Delaware River

Executive Branch

Fallingwater

Firefly

Flag

Benjamin Franklin

French and Indian War(s)

Gettysburg Address

Harrisburg

Independence Hall

Industry (-ies)

Johnstown Flood

Judicial Branch

Keystone

Lake Erie Plain

Legislative Branch

Lehigh Valley

Liberty Bell

Livestock

Middle Atlantic

Thomas Mifflin

Mined

Mount Davis

Mountain Laurel

William Penn

Pennsylvania Dutch Country

Philadelphia

Piedmont

Pittsburgh

Quakers

Railroad(s)

Ridge and Valley

River(s)

Betsy Ross

Scranton

Steel

Tribe(s)

Underground Railroad

Union

Valley Forge

Additional Terms

Choose as many additional terms as you would like and write them in the squares. Repeat each as desired.
Cut out the squares and randomly distribute them to the class.
Instruct the students to place their square on the center space of their card.

Clues for
Additional Terms

Write three clues for each of your additional terms.

_____ 1. 2. 3.	_____ 1. 2. 3.
_____ 1. 2. 3.	_____ 1. 2. 3.
_____ 1. 2. 3.	_____ 1. 2. 3.

Allegheny Plateau 1. The ___ consists mostly of forested uplands. It covers about 60% of the state and is part of the Appalachian Plateau. 2. The ___ covers a large part of northern and western Pennsylvania. The Pocono Mountains are in this region.	**Allentown** 1. ___ is located on the Lehigh River. It is the state's third most populous city. 2. Dorney Park and Wildwater Kingdom are located just outside of this city.
Atlantic Coastal Plain 1. The extreme southeast corner of the state is in the ___. This narrow strip of low, flat land runs parallel to the Delaware River. It falls to sea level where it meets the Delaware River. 2. Philadelphia, Delaware, and Bucks counties are in this small geographic region.	**Battle of Gettysburg** 1. This Civil War battle was fought from July 1 to July 3, 1863. It is sometimes called the turning point of the Civil War. 2. This battle had the greatest number of casualties in the Civil War.
Border(s) 1. New York, New Jersey, Delaware, Maryland, West Virginia, and Ohio ___ Pennsylvania. 2. A small part of Lake Erie ___ Pennsylvania. This is the small Central Lowlands region.	**James Buchanan** 1. ___, the fifteenth President of the United States, was born in Cove Gap, Pennsylvania. 2. Wheatland was President ___'s estate. It is near Lancaster.
Commonwealth 1. Pennsylvania is one of four states to officially use the name ___. The others are Kentucky, Massachusetts, and Virginia. 2. Complete this analogy: nation : country :: ___ : state	**County (-ies)** 1. There are 67 ___ in Pennsylvania. 2. ___ in Pennsylvania are categorized according to their population. Philadelphia is the only first-class ___.
Crop(s) 1. Pennsylvania produces a wide variety of ___. Greenhouse and nursery products, mushrooms; fruit; potatoes; and grains such as corn, wheat, and oats are important ___. 2. Top ___ in terms of revenue are greenhouse and nursery products and mushrooms.	**Declaration of Independence** 1. The ___ was signed in Philadelphia on July 4, 1776. 2. The signers of the ___ included nine representatives from Pennsylvania. Among them were Benjamin Franklin, Robert Morris, and Benjamin Rush.

Pennsylvania Bingo

Delaware River
1. The ___ cuts an S-shaped pass through the mountains, forming the Delaware Water Gap. 2. The ___ forms the entire border with New Jersey and part of the border with New York.

Executive Branch
1. The ___ of government enforces laws. It comprises the governor, the lt. governor, the attorney general, the auditor general, the state treasurer, the secretary of education, and several agencies.
2. The governor is head of the ___. The present-day governor is [fill in].

Fallingwater
1. Famed architect Frank Lloyd Wright designed ___. He also designed Duncan House and Kentuck Knob. All 3 homes are in the Laurel Highlands.
2. ___ is dramatically cantilevered over a waterfall and widely considered to be Frank Lloyd Wright's best work.

Firefly
1. The ___ is the official insect of Pennsylvania.
2. This insect produces light through a chemical reaction using special photic organs.

Flag
1. The state coat of arms is on a blue field on both sides of the state ___. Symbols include a ship, a plow, 3 sheaves of wheat, an eagle, a stalk of corn, and an olive branch.
2. The state ___ has the state motto: "Virtue, Liberty, and Independence."

Benjamin Franklin
1. ___ was an author, printer, politician, scientist, musician, inventor, satirist, statesman, and diplomat. He was also the first United States Postmaster General.
2. He published *Poor Richard's Almanack* using the pseudonym Richard Saunders.

French and Indian War(s)
1. The ___ refers to the main enemies of the British colonists during the conflict: the French forces and their Native American allies. Both the English and the French claimed the land west of the Appalachian Mountains.
2. The ___ officially ended with the signing of the Treaty of Paris on February 10, 1763.

Gettysburg Address
1. President Lincoln delivered the ___ at the dedication of the Soldiers' National Cemetery.
2. The ___ begins, "Four score and twenty years ago…" This line referred to the signing of the Declaration of Independence.

Harrisburg
1. ___ is the capital of Pennsylvania.
2. ___ lies on the east bank of the Susquehanna River. The Pennsylvania Farm Show takes place every year in this city.

Independence Hall
1. ___ is in Philadelphia. The Liberty Bell, which was once in its tower, now stands in front of it.
2. Many important events took place in this building. Among them were the adoption of the Declaration of Independence and the drafting of the U. S. Constitution.

Pennsylvania Bingo

Industry (-ies) 1. Chemicals, steel, farming , mining, electronics equipment, cars, and pharmaceuticals are important ___. 2. Food processing is an important ___. Important products include beer; bread and cakes; chocolate and cocoa products; cookies, crackers, and pretzels; and sausages and prepared meats.	**Johnstown Flood** 1. This catastrophe of 1889 was caused by the failure of the South Fork Dam. About 20,000,000 tons of water were released as a result. 2. More than 2,200 people died as a result of this disaster.
Judicial Branch 1. The ___ interprets what our laws mean and makes decisions about the laws and those who break them. 2. The ___ of state government is made up of several courts, the highest of which is the state Supreme Court.	**Keystone** 1. The state's nickname has been "The ___ State" since about 1800. 2. A ___ is the central, wedge-shaped stone in an arch; it holds all the other stones in place.
Lake Erie Plain 1. The ___ comprises the small portion of northwestern Pennsylvania along Lake Erie. 2. Erie, the fourth largest city in the state, is in this small, narrow region.	**Legislative Branch** 1. The General Assembly is the ___ of government; it comprises the Senate and the House of Representatives. 2. The ___ makes the laws.
Lehigh Valley 1. Three cities in the ___ are Allentown, Bethlehem, and Easton. 2. This region is named for the river which runs through it; it is part of the Great [Appalachian] Valley.	**Liberty Bell** 1. Visitors to Philadelphia often go to see this symbol of American independence. 2. Its inscription reads, "Proclaim LIBERTY throughout all the Land unto all the Inhabitants thereof."
Livestock 1. ___ products, including dairy products, are important to the state's economy. Milk production is the leading segment of the agricultural industry. 2. The sale of ___ and ___ products accounts for 69% of Pennsylvania's farm income.	**Middle Atlantic** 1. Pennsylvania is in the __ Region of the United States. 2. Most sources include New Jersey, New York, Pennsylvania, Delaware, and Maryland in this region.

Pennsylvania Bingo

Thomas Mifflin	Mined
1. ___ was the first governor of the state of Pennsylvania 2. He held the office of governor from 1790 to 1799.	1. Important ___ products include coal, petroleum, and natural gas. Limestone, sand, and slate are also ___. 2. Coal has been ___ in Pennsylvania since the mid 1700s. Much of it is used for the generation of electric power.
Mount Davis 1. At 3,213 feet, ___ is the highest point in the state. I 2. ___, the highest point in the state, is in Forbes State Forest, which is in the Laurel Highlands in the Allegheny Mountains.	**Mountain Laurel** 1. The blossom of the ___ is the state flower. 2. This beautiful evergreen shrub has pink and white blossoms.
William Penn 1. ___ founded the Province of Pennsylvania, also known as Pennsylvania Colony. 2. ___ designed a government dedicated to religious freedom and democratic principles.	**Pennsylvania Dutch Country** 1. Lancaster and the surrounding area is often referred to as ___. 2. Many visit this area because of the Amish settlement, where thousands still live a centuries-old "Plain" lifestyle.
Philadelphia 1. This city was the site of the First Continental Congress, the Second Continental Congress, and the Constitutional Convention. 2. ___ is the largest city in Pennsylvania. It is in the Atlantic Coastal Plain.	**Piedmont** 1. The ___ is west of the Atlantic Coastal Plain. 2. The ___ is between the flat Coastal Plain and the Appalachian mountain system. It is an area of gently rolling foothills.
Pittsburgh 1. Point State Park in ___ is built on the former site of Fort Duquesne. 2. The Allegheny and Monongahela rivers meet in ___ and form the Ohio River.	**Quakers** 1. Members of the Religious Society of Friends are called ___. 2. Although many English Anglicans settled in the area as well, the English ___ were the dominant group of settlers to inhabit the Province of Pennsylvania.

Pennsylvania Bingo

Railroad(s) 1. Founded in 1846 as in-state line, the Pennsylvania ___ became the nation's most important ___. 2. ___ gave the North a major advantage over the Confederacy during the Civil War.	**Ridge and Valley** 1. The ___ region consists of a series of fertile valleys and long, parallel ridges that are part of the Appalachian Mountain range. 2. The Great Valley is in the ___ region. It comprises Lebanon, Lehigh, and Cumberland valleys. Blue Mountain, Tuscarora, and Jack's Mountain are in this region.
River(s) 1. The Allegheny, Susquehanna, Delaware, Monongahela, and Ohio are important ___ in Pennsylvania. 2. There are 45,000 miles of ___ and streams in the state.	**Betsy Ross** 1. This upholsterer is credited with designing the American flag. 2. Her house can be seen on Arch Street in Philadelphia.
Scranton 1. ___ and Wilkes-Barre form the metropolitan area of the Wyoming Valley. 2. ___ is the sixth largest city after Philadelphia, Pittsburgh, Allentown, Erie, and Reading.	**Steel** 1. ___ is an alloy made by combining iron and carbon or other elements. 2. For about 100 years, Pennsylvania was the "___ Capital of the World." This was due to the state's rich deposits of bituminous, or soft, coal and iron ore.
Tribe(s) 1. Algonkian and Iroquoian ___ lived in the area before the Europeans arrived. 2. Algonkian ___ included the Delaware, Nanticoke, and Shawnee. The Susquehannocks, an Iroquoian ___, lived along the Susquehanna River.	**Underground Railroad** 1. William Still was a conductor on the ___. He helped nearly 800 former slaves escape. 2. As part of the ___, Philadelphia's network of abolitionists helped more than 100 slaves escape each year.
Union 1. Pennsylvania was the second state to enter the Union. 2. During the American Revolutionary War, Pennsylvania fought on the ___ side. Pennsylvania Bingo	**Valley Forge** 1. The American Continental Army spent the winter of 1777–1778 at ___. 2. Baron von Steuben, a Prussian officer, helped train General Washington's troops at ___.

Pennsylvania Bingo

Piedmont	Allegheny Plateau	Atlantic Coastal Plain	Harrisburg	Border(s)
French and Indian War(s)	Allentown	Underground Railroad	Industry (-ies)	Railroad(s)
Tribe(s)	Livestock		William Penn	Union
Steel	Quakers	Scranton	Liberty Bell	Thomas Mifflin
Mount Davis	Judicial Branch	Firefly	River(s)	Mountain Laurel

Pennsylvania Bingo

Steel	Tribe(s)	Lake Erie Plain	Pittsburgh	Lehigh Valley
Thomas Mifflin	Flag	County (-ies)	Quakers	Mined
Declaration of Independence	Judicial Branch		Keystone	Scranton
Pennsylvania Dutch Country	Philadelphia	Livestock	Valley Forge	Border(s)
Railroad(s)	Underground Railroad	Firefly	French and Indian War(s)	River(s)

Pennsylvania Bingo

Judicial Branch	Scranton	Flag	Liberty Bell	Tribe(s)
Thomas Mifflin	Allentown	Crop(s)	Allegheny Plateau	Johnstown Flood
Quakers	Underground Railroad		Mined	Battle of Gettysburg
Livestock	Declaration of Independence	Mount Davis	Pennsylvania Dutch Country	Lake Erie Plain
River(s)	Delaware River	Firefly	Valley Forge	Lehigh Valley

Pennsylvania Bingo

Livestock	Mined	Atlantic Coastal Plain	Delaware River	Lehigh Valley
Middle Atlantic	Commonwealth	Allegheny Plateau	Pittsburgh	Tribe(s)
William Penn	Pennsylvania Dutch Country		Mountain Laurel	Harrisburg
Scranton	Allentown	Underground Railroad	Firefly	County (-ies)
Executive Branch	Railroad(s)	James Buchanan	River(s)	Union

Pennsylvania Bingo

Railroad(s)	Border(s)	Quakers	County (-ies)	Delaware River
Middle Atlantic	Scranton	Crop(s)	Keystone	Allentown
Atlantic Coastal Plain	Union		Industry (-ies)	Independence Hall
Mountain Laurel	Lehigh Valley	Piedmont	Valley Forge	Fallingwater
Flag	Firefly	Tribe(s)	Livestock	William Penn

Pennsylvania Bingo

Battle of Gettysburg	Mined	Lake Erie Plain	Lehigh Valley	Union
Liberty Bell	Quakers	Fallingwater	Allegheny Plateau	Tribe(s)
Pittsburgh	Executive Branch		Commonwealth	Keystone
Firefly	Mount Davis	Valley Forge	James Buchanan	Atlantic Coastal Plain
Thomas Mifflin	County (-ies)	Piedmont	William Penn	Benjamin Franklin

Pennsylvania Bingo

Piedmont	Mined	Independence Hall	Scranton	Flag
Thomas Mifflin	Lehigh Valley	Judicial Branch	Allentown	Middle Atlantic
Union	Harrisburg		Keystone	Commonwealth
Livestock	Pennsylvania Dutch Country	Crop(s)	Steel	Declaration of Independence
Firefly	Delaware River	Valley Forge	James Buchanan	Battle of Gettysburg

Pennsylvania Bingo

William Penn	Mined	Gettysburg Address	Liberty Bell	Commonwealth
Middle Atlantic	Atlantic Coastal Plain	Pittsburgh	Union	County (-ies)
Benjamin Franklin	Delaware River		Lehigh Valley	Border(s)
River(s)	Livestock	Steel	Executive Branch	Pennsylvania Dutch Country
Underground Railroad	Firefly	James Buchanan	Quakers	Thomas Mifflin

Pennsylvania Bingo: Card No. 8

Pennsylvania Bingo

Keystone	Flag	Judicial Branch	Benjamin Franklin	Delaware River
Executive Branch	Lehigh Valley	William Penn	Quakers	Mined
Johnstown Flood	Piedmont		Allentown	Gettysburg Address
Fallingwater	Border(s)	Mount Davis	Industry (-ies)	Independence Hall
Pennsylvania Dutch Country	Valley Forge	Crop(s)	Steel	Mountain Laurel

Pennsylvania Bingo

Steel	Liberty Bell	Commonwealth	Pittsburgh	Benjamin Franklin
Union	County (-ies)	Allegheny Plateau	Allentown	Lehigh Valley
Delaware River	Mined		Harrisburg	Declaration of Independence
Mount Davis	Mountain Laurel	Fallingwater	Valley Forge	Johnstown Flood
Crop(s)	Thomas Mifflin	Lake Erie Plain	Railroad(s)	William Penn

Pennsylvania Bingo

Battle of Gettysburg	Mined	Quakers	Fallingwater	Thomas Mifflin
Gettysburg Address	Johnstown Flood	Industry (-ies)	Keystone	Allegheny Plateau
Middle Atlantic	Lehigh Valley		Lake Erie Plain	Judicial Branch
Crop(s)	Tribe(s)	Valley Forge	Delaware River	Steel
Executive Branch	Firefly	Piedmont	James Buchanan	Flag

Pennsylvania Bingo

Flag	Border(s)	Johnstown Flood	Liberty Bell	Keystone
Judicial Branch	Thomas Mifflin	Atlantic Coastal Plain	James Buchanan	Allentown
Piedmont	Independence Hall		Union	Pittsburgh
Firefly	Pennsylvania Dutch Country	Lehigh Valley	Steel	Middle Atlantic
Mined	Gettysburg Address	Delaware River	Executive Branch	County (-ies)

Pennsylvania Bingo

Fallingwater	Border(s)	Battle of Gettysburg	Johnstown Flood	Union
Atlantic Coastal Plain	Gettysburg Address	Lehigh Valley	Keystone	Declaration of Independence
Liberty Bell	County (-ies)		Judicial Branch	Independence Hall
William Penn	Valley Forge	Commonwealth	Delaware River	Steel
Firefly	Mountain Laurel	James Buchanan	Piedmont	Industry (-ies)

Pennsylvania Bingo: Card No. 13

Pennsylvania Bingo

French and Indian War(s)	Lehigh Valley	Quakers	Keystone	Executive Branch
County (-ies)	Piedmont	Johnstown Flood	Allentown	Mined
Fallingwater	Harrisburg		Lake Erie Plain	Crop(s)
Mountain Laurel	Valley Forge	Delaware River	Commonwealth	Battle of Gettysburg
Firefly	Pittsburgh	Declaration of Independence	Thomas Mifflin	William Penn

Pennsylvania Bingo

Industry (-ies)	Keystone	Quakers	Flag	Liberty Bell
Battle of Gettysburg	Lake Erie Plain	Allegheny Plateau	Atlantic Coastal Plain	Executive Branch
Union	Piedmont		Tribe(s)	Mined
Firefly	Johnstown Flood	Gettysburg Address	Valley Forge	Fallingwater
Thomas Mifflin	Pennsylvania Dutch Country	James Buchanan	Benjamin Franklin	Judicial Branch

Pennsylvania Bingo

Commonwealth	Johnstown Flood	Gettysburg Address	Benjamin Franklin	Philadelphia
Pittsburgh	Declaration of Independence	Independence Hall	Middle Atlantic	Harrisburg
Fallingwater	Border(s)		Union	Judicial Branch
Livestock	County (-ies)	Firefly	Industry (-ies)	Steel
Executive Branch	Betsy Ross	James Buchanan	Pennsylvania Dutch Country	Mined

Pennsylvania Bingo

Crop(s)	Ridge and Valley	Legislative Branch	Johnstown Flood	French and Indian War(s)
Industry (-ies)	Executive Branch	Valley Forge	Harrisburg	Independence Hall
Keystone	William Penn		Betsy Ross	Gettysburg Address
Mountain Laurel	Thomas Mifflin	Steel	Quakers	Declaration of Independence
Mount Davis	Fallingwater	Flag	Liberty Bell	Border(s)

Pennsylvania Bingo

Benjamin Franklin	Delaware River	County (-ies)	Fallingwater	Pittsburgh
Mined	Crop(s)	Mount Davis	Union	Executive Branch
Keystone	Declaration of Independence			Atlantic Coastal Plain
Border(s)	Allegheny Plateau	Valley Forge	Steel	Lake Erie Plain
Betsy Ross	Johnstown Flood	Quakers	Ridge and Valley	Battle of Gettysburg

Pennsylvania Bingo

Union	Battle of Gettysburg	Johnstown Flood	Gettysburg Address	Steel
Industry (-ies)	Liberty Bell	Mined	Flag	Harrisburg
Ridge and Valley	Delaware River		Allentown	Tribe(s)
Lake Erie Plain	Betsy Ross	Mount Davis	Pennsylvania Dutch Country	Legislative Branch
Atlantic Coastal Plain	Philadelphia	Thomas Mifflin	William Penn	James Buchanan

Pennsylvania Bingo

French and Indian War(s)	Ridge and Valley	Liberty Bell	Johnstown Flood	James Buchanan
County (-ies)	Judicial Branch	Middle Atlantic	Mount Davis	Pittsburgh
Border(s)	Independence Hall		Livestock	Allegheny Plateau
Railroad(s)	Underground Railroad	River(s)	Pennsylvania Dutch Country	Betsy Ross
Scranton	William Penn	Philadelphia	Steel	Legislative Branch

Pennsylvania Bingo

Industry (-ies)	Battle of Gettysburg	Middle Atlantic	Johnstown Flood	Railroad(s)
Border(s)	Legislative Branch	Commonwealth	Gettysburg Address	Piedmont
Declaration of Independence	Thomas Mifflin		Ridge and Valley	Quakers
Mount Davis	Flag	Betsy Ross	Mountain Laurel	William Penn
Livestock	Philadelphia	James Buchanan	Crop(s)	Pennsylvania Dutch Country

Pennsylvania Bingo

Benjamin Franklin	Lake Erie Plain	Legislative Branch	Atlantic Coastal Plain	Fallingwater
Pittsburgh	Liberty Bell	Tribe(s)	Gettysburg Address	Allentown
County (-ies)	Harrisburg		Piedmont	Independence Hall
Betsy Ross	Mountain Laurel	Pennsylvania Dutch Country	Allegheny Plateau	Middle Atlantic
Philadelphia	Crop(s)	Ridge and Valley	Declaration of Independence	Livestock

Pennsylvania Bingo

Commonwealth	Ridge and Valley	Flag	Atlantic Coastal Plain	James Buchanan
Battle of Gettysburg	French and Indian War(s)	Thomas Mifflin	Industry (-ies)	Allegheny Plateau
Lake Erie Plain	Fallingwater		River(s)	Piedmont
Declaration of Independence	Philadelphia	Betsy Ross	Crop(s)	Pennsylvania Dutch Country
Railroad(s)	Underground Railroad	William Penn	Mount Davis	Legislative Branch

Pennsylvania Bingo

Commonwealth	William Penn	French and Indian War(s)	Ridge and Valley	Gettysburg Address
Legislative Branch	James Buchanan	Middle Atlantic	Pittsburgh	Piedmont
Independence Hall	Benjamin Franklin		Fallingwater	Declaration of Independence
Railroad(s)	River(s)	Betsy Ross	Crop(s)	Border(s)
Scranton	Livestock	Philadelphia	Liberty Bell	Underground Railroad

Pennsylvania Bingo

Livestock	Middle Atlantic	Ridge and Valley	Quakers	Legislative Branch
Allegheny Plateau	Border(s)	Industry (-ies)	Commonwealth	Allentown
Mountain Laurel	Gettysburg Address		River(s)	Betsy Ross
Tribe(s)	Railroad(s)	Underground Railroad	Philadelphia	Harrisburg
James Buchanan	French and Indian War(s)	County (-ies)	Executive Branch	Scranton

Pennsylvania Bingo: Card No. 25

Pennsylvania Bingo

Legislative Branch	Ridge and Valley	Lake Erie Plain	Pittsburgh	Benjamin Franklin
Mount Davis	Liberty Bell	Gettysburg Address	French and Indian War(s)	Commonwealth
Mountain Laurel	River(s)		Harrisburg	Livestock
Crop(s)	Atlantic Coastal Plain	Railroad(s)	Philadelphia	Betsy Ross
Independence Hall	Executive Branch	Quakers	Underground Railroad	Scranton

Pennsylvania Bingo

Lake Erie Plain	County (-ies)	Ridge and Valley	French and Indian War(s)	Judicial Branch
Railroad(s)	River(s)	Industry (-ies)	Betsy Ross	Allentown
Valley Forge	Underground Railroad		Philadelphia	Livestock
Benjamin Franklin	Battle of Gettysburg	Middle Atlantic	Scranton	Allegheny Plateau
Executive Branch	Harrisburg	Legislative Branch	Tribe(s)	Independence Hall

Pennsylvania Bingo

Lake Erie Plain	French and Indian War(s)	Tribe(s)	Ridge and Valley	Commonwealth
Judicial Branch	Legislative Branch	River(s)	Pittsburgh	Harrisburg
Underground Railroad	Declaration of Independence		Independence Hall	Mount Davis
Steel	Benjamin Franklin	Thomas Mifflin	Philadelphia	Betsy Ross
Atlantic Coastal Plain	Keystone	Executive Branch	Scranton	Railroad(s)

Pennsylvania Bingo

Legislative Branch	French and Indian War(s)	Benjamin Franklin	Industry (-ies)	Keystone
Pennsylvania Dutch Country	Mount Davis	Middle Atlantic	Independence Hall	Tribe(s)
Mountain Laurel	River(s)		Allentown	Ridge and Valley
Judicial Branch	Railroad(s)	Lehigh Valley	Philadelphia	Betsy Ross
Commonwealth	Gettysburg Address	Scranton	Battle of Gettysburg	Underground Railroad

Pennsylvania Bingo: Card No. 29

Pennsylvania Bingo

Delaware River	Ridge and Valley	Pittsburgh	Keystone	Betsy Ross
Allegheny Plateau	French and Indian War(s)	Lake Erie Plain	Harrisburg	Allentown
Mountain Laurel	Fallingwater		Independence Hall	Middle Atlantic
Scranton	Battle of Gettysburg	Atlantic Coastal Plain	Philadelphia	River(s)
Railroad(s)	Union	Underground Railroad	Legislative Branch	Tribe(s)

Pennsylvania Bingo: Card No. 30

© Barbara M. Peller

www.ingramcontent.com/pod-product-compliance
Lightning Source LLC
LaVergne TN
LVHW061341060426
835511LV00014B/2057